This book is dedicated to my mother,
Denise Rickman (nee O'Farrell), whose warm
and encouraging smile picked me up and
calmed me down in equal measure.

The Little
Book of
Serenity

Cheryl Rickman

An Hachette UK Company
www.hachette.co.uk

First published in Great Britain in 2020 by Gaia Books,
an imprint of Octopus Publishing Group Ltd
Carmelite House
50 Victoria Embankment
London EC4Y 0DZ
www.octopusbooks.co.uk

Distributed in the US by Hachette Book Group,
1290 Avenue of the Americas, 4th and 5th Floors, New York, NY 10104

Distributed in Canada by Canadian Manda Group,
664 Annette Street, Toronto, Ontario, Canada M6S 2C8

ISBN 978-1-85675-421-7

A CIP catalogue record for this book is available from the British Library.

Printed and bound in China.

10 9 8 7 6 5 4 3 2 1

Publishing Director: Stephanie Jackson
Art Director: Juliette Norsworthy
Senior Editor: Pollyanna Poulter
Designer and Illustrator: Abi Read
Copy Editor: Alison Wormleighton
Senior Production Controller: Allison Gonsalves

Contents

Introduction 6

1. Serenity ABC 9

2. Serene Mind:
Thoughts and Feelings 20

3. The Pause 42

4. Self-calm:
12 Nourishing Actions 60

Conclusion 95

Acknowledgements 96

Introduction

Overwhelmed? Under pressure? You're not alone. The strife of modern life can get on top of us all. And it's no wonder.

We're distracted by a dizzying array of deadlines, chores and social feeds that relentlessly take us away from calm. The buzz of busyness keeps us on edge as we worry about whether we've missed something we were meant to do.

Consequently, many of us are like the proverbial swan – appearing serene, yet paddling like crazy underwater.

Serenity is not our current status quo; chaos, expectation and a rising tide of stress levels are.

The tyranny of tiredness prevails as we succumb to our never-ending to-do lists and plough through, striving, winning, losing, learning. It's exhausting.

And we can't just jack it all in and sail off into the sunset to meditate for ever. We have money to earn, mouths to feed, dreams to pursue.

But what if there were a way to find calm amid the chaos?

This book will equip you with ideas and gentle pauses to release some of life's tension and generate more ease; it is a manual to help you tackle the topsy-turviness of life.

It isn't easy. Constant connection to our electronic devices means we're permanently 'on call', yet increasingly disconnected from the moments that make up our lives.

Productivity and achievement have taken priority over serenity and contentment.

We're overloaded with a steady stream of stimulation, information and bleeping phone notifications.

It's a noisy place to live.

A rise in anxiety and depression is the global response to this piled-on pressure. And the crescendo of noise bombards our senses and fills the space where peace, quiet and downtime once lived.

The collection of wisdom across these pages aims to soften the edges of life. Peppered with intentional pauses to help lighten your responses, quieten your mind and awaken your outlook, *The Little Book of Serenity* is part antidote to pandemonium and part guide to peaceful living amid the mayhem of modern life.

The interventions explained in this book will show you how to build calm into the fabric of even the most frenetic lifestyle, and to regain a sense of balance and ease, so you may stand with confidence at the helm of your boat, navigating stormy seas towards calmer waters.

As you introduce some peaceful practices and mindful moments, you'll be able to put up less resistance and to flow with greater ease along the river of life.

And. Just. Breathe.

'Though the bamboo forest is dense, water flows through it freely.'

Zen proverb

1. Serenity ABC

When faced with difficult situations, we have two choices: we can either change them or we can change how we look at them. Given that much of what happens to us is outside of our control, the first option isn't always possible.

So, I wonder...

What if we viewed whatever's outside our control with calm acceptance rather than fierce resistance?

What if we chose to let go of past regrets, shook off future worries and focused on what we *can* control?

What if we accepted that our own personal experience matters more than someone else's opinion?

What if we recognized the pressure of perfection for what it is – impossible – and accepted ourselves as enough?

What if we accepted the whole spectrum of our emotions – from happiness to sadness and everything in between?

What if we viewed our lives through the 'ABC' lens of acceptance, balance and compassion, rather than comparison, criticism and expectation?

Surely we'd enjoy a calmer journey along the river of life? Not always, but often.

This chapter outlines some of the ways to practise accepting the inevitable challenges of life and find a healthy balance between growth and gratitude, between self-improvement and self-acceptance, between betterment and contentment.

'The best thing one can do when it is raining is let it rain.'

Henry Wadsworth Longfellow

Acceptance

Sometimes plans get thwarted, expectations go
unmet and mistakes are made, so we experience
discomfort. Yet these are the times when we learn
the most about ourselves; the times to practise
acceptance and stay open to learning, to control
what we can and to flow with what we can't.

- **Expect the best, and accept or change the worst**.
  Expectation can lead to disappointment, but that's no
  reason not to expect good things to happen. Leading with
  hope and positive expectation creates a good feeling and
  can attract the best outcome. However, if things *don't* go to
  plan, we can let go and accept the situation (if it can't be
  changed) or do something about it (if it can be changed).
  Maybe it wasn't meant to be, right now. Or perhaps it's
  signalling the need to change course.

- **Accept your own flaws**. Accepting and celebrating our
  differences and imperfections lessens the pressure of social
  comparison and empowers us to be our unique selves
  without the exhausting task of maintaining a facade. You
  can then balance this self-acceptance by considering and
  celebrating your unique strengths.

- **Remind yourself that everything counts.** Even failures and mistakes have value, as long as we learn from them. In fact, discomfort is a far better teacher than comfort is, because we learn so much more about ourselves when things go wrong than when they go right. We wouldn't learn much if everything always ran smoothly. Knowing that everything counts makes failing more valuable and less daunting, and it helps us accept uncomfortable moments as they arise.

- **Notice and accept or act.** If you get wound up and start to resist whatever's happening, do the following:

  1. Decide whether the situation causing that reaction is within your control or not.

  2. If it *is* within your control, do something about it or roll with it: these are the options for leading a calm life.

  3. If it *isn't* within your control, consider whether there's anything you can learn from the situation that might help you keep your cool the next time you face something similar. For example, you can't prevent poor weather on your wedding day, but you could practise spotting the silver lining (for example, noticing the

camaraderie among your guests as they huddle together under umbrellas and canopies). You can't control your teenager's mood swings, but you can control how you respond, whether walking away and choosing to talk when they're calmer, suggesting you each drink some water (giving you both a chance to calm down) or making their favourite dinner with a 'Can we start again?' note on the side, to demonstrate your love, however it's received. (And give yourself permission to be human when you *don't* respond in that way.)

Balance

Creating serenity in our lives involves balancing
how we spend our time and what we choose to do.

- **Routinely plan your week and decide on three
  key tasks you aim to complete.** Prioritizing a few
  important actions makes it easier to accept when you
  don't manage to complete everything on your list. There's
  always tomorrow, and taking some action equals progress.

- **Leave space in your schedule for wiggle room.**
  This is crucial to give you flexibility in case the goalposts
  are moved.

- **Know what your big rocks are.** See your life as a jar
  in which you can place big rocks, small pebbles and sand.
  The big rocks are the things that matter most because they
  nourish your soul (family, exercise, solitude, friendships,
  creativity). The small pebbles are the relatively important
  things (work tasks, paying bills), and the grains of sand are
  the less critical parts (ironing, watching TV). Fill the jar
  with sand or small pebbles and you'll have no room for
  the big rocks: no room for what matters most. So list your
  big rocks to allow you to find a healthy balance between

work, life, family, friends, hobbies and health. The aim is to create space for activities that feed your soul, which in turn will give you enough energy to move productively through your to-do list.

Compassion

We're all in this together, so give yourself and those around you permission to be human.

- **Notice how well you've done rather than what you've done wrong.** Balance an acceptance of what you've achieved with a commitment to learn from your mistakes. Trying to be flawless is hopeless, and the quest to be the best is exhausting. So give yourself a break and a pat on the back for each and every small achievement.

- **Be warm and gentle with yourself.** Practise being your own best ally, rather than your own worst enemy. Ask yourself what you need, just as you might ask a friend who's struggling. What can you offer? Reassurance? Forgiveness? Encouragement? A good long walk?

- **Find a photograph of yourself as a baby and another of your ten-year-old self.** The next time you hear your inner critic ranting, imagine it's speaking to that baby or child. That's still you. Your inner child remains within you – so be kind. Keep that photograph as a reminder to speak with encouragement and acceptance rather than harsh criticism and judgement.

- **Put your hand on your heart and say, 'It's OK'.**
  This response taps into the three main triggers of the
  physiological compassion system: gentle touch, physical
  warmth and soothing vocalization. Your physiology literally
  calms down while activating your inner caregiving system.

- **Remind yourself that we all make mistakes.** How
  we view ourselves and humanity can dramatically impact
  how we relate to failure and how often we respond with
  compassion to getting things wrong. With self-esteem we
  only feel good when we succeed, but self-compassion also
  works when we fail, as it's not about seeing ourselves in a
  positive light only when we're doing well.

When we view our lives
through the 'ABC' lens of
acceptance, balance and
compassion – both for
ourselves and for others – we
become better equipped to
cope with, and cherish, life in
all its occasionally brutal glory.
And this makes for serenity.

2.

Serene Mind: Thoughts and Feelings

What we *think*, *feel* and *do* influences how calm we are. Positive thoughts and feelings are critical to cultivating a state of serenity, so the more we worry, judge and complain, the less serene we become, while the more we gain perspective, feel grateful and savour life, the calmer we will be.

What we fill our minds with determines whether we feel calm or overwhelmed.

Our rational brains are often hijacked by irrational reactions, which don't serve us well. Yet we tend only to realize with hindsight that we needn't have fretted so much.

The problem is…we are wired to worry.

'I've suffered a great many catastrophes in my life. Most of them never happened.'

Michel de Montaigne

Back in the days when we lived in caves, when sunlight woke us and we thrived outside, our intuition guided us, so our tendency to worry first and ask questions later was very useful. It alerted us to and protected us from the life-threatening dangers that lurked around every corner. Today, these life-or-death dangers no longer exist, yet our default 'what if' wiring remains.

It's part of our evolutionary biology to worry despite no longer requiring protection from sabre-toothed tigers. What's more, we now know that worry doesn't help us perform better, achieve things faster or solve whatever problems we're worrying about – it makes the present less enjoyable.

Thankfully, we have it within us to get ourselves from worked up to calmed down and, in doing so, bolster our problem-solving capacity.

Tackling Worries

We worry about what others think of us – yet
they're just worrying about what we think of
them. We worry about whether we'll achieve
our desired future or whether it will all go
wrong – yet this pressure to succeed hampers us.
Ironically, the more we worry, the less able we
are to solve the problems we're worrying about.

A serene state of mind will more
readily facilitate our ability to
impress/succeed/cope than
a frenzied one. When we get
stressed and anxious, we can't
access our logical, rational brain.
The part of the brain known
as the amygdala goes on red
alert and refuses to let logical
thoughts through, instead
focusing on bringing our
fight-or-flight response online.

When we're stressed or anxious,
the only way to let rational thoughts
through is to get calm.

Think Clearly

Serenity literally opens our minds, which improves clarity and decision-making, enabling us to make choices based on logic rather than emotion. So, in our quest to do well, it is better to calm down so we can open up.

Whenever we worry about what *might* happen, we tend to overestimate threats and underestimate how well we'll cope.

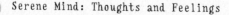

In fact, what we fear might happen often doesn't, or if it does, we cope far better than we expected to. We rarely give ourselves credit for our levels of adaptability. Yet worrying continues to steal our joy.

So how can we stay calm in the face of fear and anxiety, and manage our thoughts rather than let them manage us?

- **Distract yourself.** Take your mind away from anxious thoughts and worries by focusing on a cognitive task, such as counting clouds or naming animals.

- **Gain perspective.** Consider the worst-case, best-case and most likely scenarios for what you're worried about. Give a probability percentage to each. Create an action plan to achieve the most likely scenario and smile about how far-fetched and unlikely the worst- and best-case scenarios were. Let's say you've been made redundant:

  1. Worst-case scenario: You never find another job, your house is repossessed and you end up homeless and penniless (2 per cent).

2. Best-case scenario: You start your own company and become a millionaire (2 per cent).

3. Most likely scenario: You talk to your mortgage company to get a payment holiday, find another (actually better) job or start a business and wind up earning more than your previous job paid (96 per cent).

- **Remind yourself of all the times you've coped better than you expected.** By considering what you've been through, how hardships have shaped you, taught you and made you who you are, you remind yourself that, whatever happens, you'll survive.

- **Remember that you'll learn more when things go wrong than when things go right.** The cliché is true – what doesn't break you really does make you stronger.

- **Jot down everything you worried about today.** Will you still be worrying about those things in a year's time?

- **Schedule in 'worry time'.** Allocate a time each day to sit down and give your worries some calm consideration. Find a solution, create a plan of action or postpone them until tomorrow and get a good night's sleep.

- **Remind yourself that uncertainty brings with it possibility.** And remember, there's little point trying to avoid uncertainty when you can't know or control what will happen in the future.

- **Be yourself.** Don't waste time worrying about what other people think of you when, in reality, they're not thinking about you at all.

- **Do whatever scares you.** Fear-based overthinking causes analysis paralysis and will get you nowhere. Conversely, action cures indecision.

- **Take one step at a time towards your goals.** The controlling mind is compelled to look forwards and get way ahead of itself. So, rather than rush ahead, plan one small action you can take tomorrow.

- **Trust your subconscious mind.** It's an expert in figuring out solutions, so let it do so.

- **Release your need to control a specific outcome.** Releasing an emotional attachment to a certain expectation decreases tension.

- **Remove time limitations.** Feeling like you need to do or achieve something within a certain time period creates pressure. Letting go of the time limit releases the pressure. You can still work towards achieving your goals, but losing the deadline gives you a lifeline towards calm.

- **Embrace change.** Whether you embrace change or resist it, it will still happen; it's an inevitability of life. Choose to be at peace.

- **Reframe nervousness.** That funny feeling of butterflies that comes with being nervous is almost identical to the feeling of being excited. By saying, 'This is so exciting! What an adventure,' you can shift that nervous feeling into something positive.

- **Replace 'what if' by focusing on 'what is'.**
  Ruminating over past regrets and worrying about what might happen in the future prevents enjoyment of the here-and-now. You can't change what's happened, nor can you know what will happen in the future – all you have control over is this moment and how you respond to it.

The Plants
We Water

**Imagine that the mind
is a garden and we can
choose to water either
the flowers or the weeds.**

Habitually practising
gratitude waters the flowers, whereas habitually complaining
waters the weeds. Delighted by blessings or bogged down by
burdens – it's our choice. We hold the watering can.

Grateful thoughts lead to grateful feelings. Positive thinking,
and the resultant feeling of gratitude, benefits our nervous
system. It keeps us feeling calm and happy. Perhaps this is
why gratitude is known as 'nature's antidepressant', as studies
show it optimizes our mental and physical state.

When we focus our minds on all that we don't have, we
never have enough, but when we focus on all that we do
have, we realize we have enough – we *are* enough – and we
feel more grateful and serene as a result.

In this way, gratitude helps us step off the treadmill of continually striving for the next thing. Stepping away from that notion of 'I'll be happy when...' will allow us to enjoy what we have, decreasing our stress levels and enhancing our day-to-day experiences as we savour each moment.

The Science of What We Think

According to neuroscientific studies, practising intentional gratitude increases the amount of the positive brain chemicals oxytocin and dopamine and re-sculpts the brain by laying down more positive neural pathways (thought patterns). In other words, it trains the brain to find the silver lining in the darkest clouds.

The Science of What We Feel

Positive psychologists – specialists in the field of positive psychology – have found that gratitude deposits into our 'positivity bank account' reserves of positive emotion, which can be used during darker periods, bolstering our resilience.

Practising and Savouring Gratitude

As positive thoughts and emotions are vital to our state of serenity, here's how to get better at practising gratitude, step-by-step:

1. **Find and think about the good.** Actively seek and notice what is good in your life, in your day, in this moment. Regularly focus your attention on what you have to be grateful for.

2. **Notice how that gratitude feels in your body.** Put your hand over your heart and close your eyes.

3. **Savour that feeling of gratitude.** Aim for five to ten seconds of feeling that sense of deep gratitude flow through you.

4. **Record your gratitude.** Take photographs to capture good moments in a photo album. Write your appreciation in a gratitude journal or on sticky notes to keep in a gratitude jar. Say thank you to someone, write a thank you card or letter, visit someone to read your thank you letter to (known as a gratitude visit). Each method enables you to feel grateful twice – first in the

moment and again when you view your album, read your journal, open your jar or recall the visit.

5. **Amplify gratitude.** Do this by anticipating the good that is yet to happen, savouring it as it happens and then reflecting on the good that has happened. For example, try the following:

- **Anticipate:** Plan future moments to savour – a holiday to look forward to, a camping weekend, a season.

- **Savour:** Say out loud, 'Life is good' whenever you want to bring attention to a specific moment and savour it. This creates a verbal savouring cue for you and others.

- **Reflect:** Look through scrapbooks and photo albums so you can reminisce on all you have to be grateful for.

Plant a Garden of Flowers

If *gratitude* is about choosing to notice, appreciate and water the flowers, *savouring* is about stopping to smell the roses; to savour life as you live it. Here are ways to practise both gratitude and savouring, and to cultivate a garden of flowers not weeds.

- **Replace 'got to' with 'get to'.** Rather than list everything you've got to do, think about how brilliant it is that you *get to* do these things. Instead of 'Humph. I've got to collect my son from school now, but I'm so busy,' think, 'Good. I *get to* collect my son from school now. Not all parents have this opportunity to connect. How lucky I am.'

- **Find the goodness in ordinary moments.** These can range from the smell of coffee as you stir your cup in the morning, to the spectacular colours of the sunset at night; from the delicious taste of the meal you've made, to the warmth of the sunshine as it falls on your face.

- **Make a savouring list.** Talk with your family about what makes you feel good – the smells you like, the sights that inspire you, sounds you enjoy. Make a list and pledge to savour those each time you hear, see, smell, feel or taste them. For example:
  - The smell of pine trees, rose bushes, freshly baked bread.
  - The feel of fresh sheets, a cooling drink, a hot shower.
  - The taste of chocolate melting, honey sweetening, lemon refreshing.

- **Remind yourself to be grateful.** Put a sticky note on the mirror or beside your bed, saying, 'I feel so grateful for…'

- **Give thanks at the dinner table.** Take turns to share one or two things that happened that day for which you feel truly grateful. Make it a habit.

- **Make a scrapbook.** Collect memories to savour and reminisce about – family events, holidays, special moments.

- **List all you're grateful for as you close your eyes to go to sleep.** You'll enter a calm and blissful state as you drift off to sleep; a wonderful way to end the day.

- **Celebrate your achievements.** At the end of each week or month, as well as writing your to-do list, write your 'ta-dah' list. Record and appreciate what you've accomplished.

- **Walk with gratitude.**
  Notice what you can see,
  hear, smell and touch as
  you walk, and consider
  why you feel grateful for
  this moment. Perhaps the
  smell of pine trees is
  invigorating; maybe feeling
  the bark on the trees makes
  you feel grounded; perhaps
  you feel grateful that you
  get to walk through this
  woodland on a Monday
  morning, because you've
  created a life that enables
  you to.

A Choice Response

Being calm isn't about the absence of chaos or concern – it's about our response to how we feel. We can choose between expression and equanimity:

Expression

When we lean into our feelings and let them flow, we feel lighter, freer and calmer afterwards. To choose expression:

- **Tune in to how you feel.** Our feelings offer clues about what matters most to us, and signal potential changes of pace or direction towards a calmer life. As such, we can use our feelings to steer us in the right direction (downstream).

- **Let your feelings out.** Don't keep calm and carry on regardless – experience your feelings, release them and move on. Keeping our feelings bottled up can cause us to blow our top and can even cause physical discomfort, including irritable bowel syndrome (IBS) and other stress-related illnesses. Pushing feelings down only means they'll resurface sometime. Ignoring feelings will lead to a lack of calm later on.

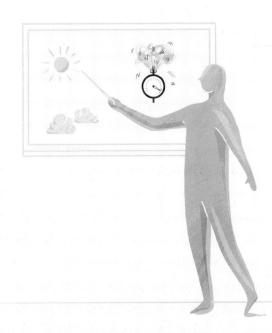

- **Label your emotions.** Studies have shown that identifying and describing an emotion activates an area of the brain known as the prefrontal cortex and decreases the intensity of the emotion. Simply by saying, 'I feel angry' or 'I feel sad', we lessen the impact and calm ourselves down.

Equanimity

We can maintain our emotional composure even as we sail the stormiest of seas and ride the waves of worry, anxiety, anger and impatience. Equanimity is a response rather than a reaction. It anchors us. To choose equanimity:

- **Use the mantra** 'this too shall pass' to remind yourself that life ebbs and flows but is never stagnant or unchanging. Pain and difficulty don't last for ever.

- **Anchor and empower yourself.** Feel yourself connected to the ground, stand tall and take a deep breath. Exhale and think, 'I am ready' as you put your hands on your hips, then extend them out to the sides or above your head. This expansive posture or 'postural feedback' is known as a 'high-power pose' and is, according to research, a way to tell your brain that you are in control.

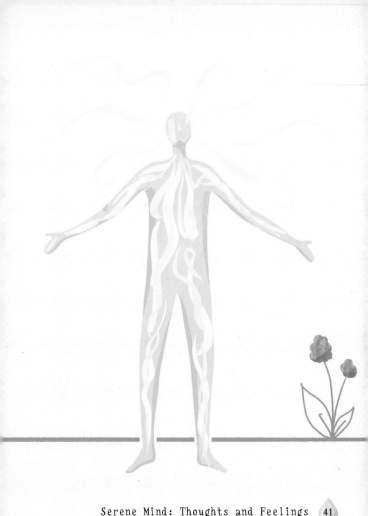

3. The Pause

In-between our thoughts, feelings and actions, in-between a situation and our reaction, is the pause. This is the place where serenity lives.

Pausing helps us tune in to that gentle sense of knowing that exists in us all, if only we paused long enough to listen to it – for the silence of the pause isn't empty; it's full of answers.

Remaining tranquil when something triggers our frustration, anger or disappointment is not always easy. Pausing *before* reacting is not our default way of being. But it can lead to a calmer response and, each time we do it, we build our capacity for sustained serenity.

'There is a voice that doesn't use words. Listen.'

Rumi

What gets in the way of the pause is our busyness. We have so much to cram into each day, and not enough time to do it all. Yet when we don't have time to do everything is precisely the best time to do nothing – to hit the pause button and rest in the present.

Stopping when we have so much to do may seem counterintuitive, but it has been proved to be beneficial. It helps us think and respond better and choose wisely. The result is an enhanced ability to plough through that to-do list with greater ease.

Embracing the In-between

How often have we all wished we'd taken a moment to pause *before* reacting? Yet in that moment, our brain has already triggered our agitated response. What can we do about this?

- **Practise pausing when you're not in fight-or-flight mode.** Pause each time you cross a threshold, each time you move from one room to another or from one activity to another. Frame the experience that is just ending before transitioning to the experience that is just beginning.

- **Pause to remind yourself of the good you've done today.** It might simply be that you got your child to school, fed yourself, replied to that email you kept putting off.

- **Stop, look up and breathe (SLUB).** Wherever you are (unless you're driving a car, obviously), try stopping, gently tipping your head back to look upwards and taking a long, deep breath in and out. This exercise, devised by the play evangelist Tanis Frame of the organization Decide to Thrive, takes just one minute to do, but opens your chest and initiates your relaxation response, providing the perfect antidote to rushing.

The Art of Mindfulness and Meditation

A busy life is a distracting one. Our default states are either being on autopilot, at our least aware, or oscillating between judgements about what *has* happened and worries about what *might* happen. Yet this restlessness reduces our enjoyment of what *is* happening – right here, right now.

Paying attention to the 'here and now' is known as mindfulness. It's the art of cultivating calm and heightened awareness of the present moment, and is an antidote to judgemental, anxious thinking. Mindfulness isn't about switching off. Rather, it is about switching *on* – to yourself and what you experience in the present moment.

All kinds of studies have proved how this inner attentiveness permanently changes the brain for the better, helping us to gain perspective, fret less and concentrate more. When we are mindful, we're less likely to jump to conclusions and more likely to make well-considered decisions.

This improved self-awareness and deeper self-connection help us respond, decide, create and think better.

Mindfulness involves two parts:

- Focusing your attention.

- Noticing your attention wandering and
  bringing it back.

When we first try mindfulness, our mind naturally jumps
from one thought to the next. So, we practise gently
bringing our attention back, over and over again.

The more you practise, the better you become at hauling
your attention back. It's a bit like pulling a helium balloon
back to float above your head. The balloon (your attention)
may drift away multiple times, but that doesn't matter. How
much you improve at pulling that balloon back is what
matters. That's mindfulness and it takes practice.

We can practise mindfulness by paying attention to our
breath, our senses and our environment and experience.

Let's explore each of these…

Mindful Breathing

When we anchor our attention to the breath, our nervous system stops pumping adrenalin and cortisol, steps down a gear from its high-alert status and becomes calmer.

Mindful breathing involves focusing your attention on the gentle inhale and exhale of your breath. It is a type of meditation, although there are many ways to do this and many breathing methods you can use. You can do it sitting, standing or lying down; with a cushion or without; with your eyes open or closed; counting as you breathe or just noticing your inhale and exhale.

The more you practise, the easier it will get, and the more you'll be able to pause and focus attention on your breath when you sense the need to calm down, find inner peace and come back to yourself.

1. **Get comfortable.** Find a stable position on a cushion or chair, sitting up straight or lying down. Rest your hands wherever they feel comfortable. Relax your body. Notice the weight of your body connecting to the chair or floor Tighten and release any areas where you feel tension.

2. **Breathe.** Inhale deeply through your nose, counting
   if you wish. Hold for a couple of seconds then exhale,
   breathing out through your mouth, again counting if
   you wish to. Tune into your breath as it flows in and
   out. There's no need to change your breathing to
   become longer or shorter – just breathe naturally.

3. **Focus.** Notice how your breath feels within your body, one breath at a time. Do you feel it in your nostrils? Your abdomen? Your throat or chest? Your tummy? Follow that sensation. Notice the point where one breath ends and the next begins. Focus on how that feels.

4. **Notice.** Your mind will wander as you become distracted by thoughts or bodily sensations. That's completely natural. Simply notice this, without any judgement, and softly say, 'Thinking'. Notice any judgements, too. Make a mental note of them, then let them pass, along with any sensations they generate in your body.

5. **Return.** Gently bring your attention back to your breath each time it drifts. Just keep pulling the balloon back. Consciously returning your attention to the present, back to your breath, gradually cultivates mindfulness. The more you can do this, the more your ability to return to your breath will increase, until it becomes second nature. That's when you will be able to deepen the sensation of being present, even when strong distractions arise.

6. **Remain.** Stay in this practice for several minutes. Continue to focus on your breath, notice your mind wandering and redirect it back to your breath. Return

your attention to your body as it sits or lies. Notice how your relaxed body feels, and feel grateful for taking this time to practise mindful breathing. Gently open your eyes.

Pausing is about noticing your life as you are living it and creating space within in-between moments. Mindfulness is about noticing your breath and bringing yourself back to it, so you can be more present in those moments. Both are ways of being *in* the moment and each enables us to take a breather.

Our breath is one of the best tools we have to cultivate a sense of serenity in our lives.

Paying Attention to Our Breath

We inhale and exhale around 20,000 times a day and yet we do so on autopilot, without noticing our breath. When we connect to our breathing, we can activate a serene state, releasing tension, suppressed emotions and toxicity as we exhale.

Try these breathing exercises to generate serenity:

- **Practise alternate nostril breathing.** Also known as Nadi Shodhana, this technique involves breathing through alternate nostrils to deepen calm. Gently rest the index and middle fingers of your right hand between your eyebrows. Press the thumb of your right hand on your right nostril to close it. Breathe through your left nostril, in and out five times. Release your thumb and press your left nostril closed using the ring finger of your right hand. Again, breathe in and out five times.

- **Speak affirmations as you breathe.** Inhale, 'I am calm'; exhale, 'All is well'.

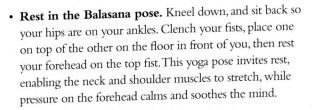

- **Rest in the Balasana pose.** Kneel down, and sit back so your hips are on your ankles. Clench your fists, place one on top of the other on the floor in front of you, then rest your forehead on the top fist. This yoga pose invites rest, enabling the neck and shoulder muscles to stretch, while pressure on the forehead calms and soothes the mind.

- **Count as you breathe.** Breathe in through your nose to the count of eight. Hold for a count of seven then breathe out through your mouth for a count of eight with your lips in a kiss-blowing position. This ancient breathing method helps the central nervous system, infusing the bloodstream with oxygen and pushing carbon dioxide from your lungs.

- **Inhale and exhale for different counts.** Distribute your breath equally between inhaling, holding your breath and exhaling: breathe in for four, hold for four, exhale for four, hold for four, then repeat. If you need a burst of oxygen, try inhaling for twice as long as you exhale: inhale for eight, exhale for four, inhale for six, exhale for three. If you're feeling anxious, try exhaling for twice as long as you inhale: inhale for four, exhale for eight, inhale for three, exhale for six.

- **Try diaphragmatic breathing.** This form of deep breathing enables you to take fuller breaths. Lie down or sit on a chair. Place your hand on your stomach and imagine a balloon inside, which expands each time you breathe in and deflates when you breathe out. Breathe in through your nose and feel your stomach press against your hand. Exhale through pursed lips; feel your stomach muscles fall inward and repeat.

- **Learn Transformational Breathing.** This is a specific technique that teaches a pattern of conscious breathing developed by Dr Judith Kravitz. Visit a Transformational Breath® coach to learn how to make better use of your respiratory system.

- **Visualize releasing negative thoughts.** Breathe in as if you are sucking up all the thoughts that are bothering you, then imagine blowing them out of your body as you exhale. Picture your thoughts in thought bubbles and breathe away your tension and worries; watch them disappear as you exhale, then inhale fresh, calm energy. Notice yourself feeling lighter.

Paying Attention to Our Senses

Focusing our attention on what we can see, hear, feel, smell and taste works well as a mindfulness strategy. This is because when we tap into our senses we give ourselves an opportunity to pause and connect to the moment.

Pause a while and notice the following:

- *Five* **things you can see.** These could include clouds in the sky, their colours and shapes and their movement.

- *Four* **things you can feel.** The surface of furniture, the texture of your clothing, the warmth of a drink are all possibilities.

- ***Three* things you can hear.** Start with sounds that are nearby, then some that are farther away and finally those that are nearby again. Are there any new sounds you didn't hear before? Also consider your internal sounds: breath, digestion, pulse.

- ***Two* things you can smell.** These might be subtle but try to describe them; it could be a mixture of scents.

- ***One* thing you can taste.** Take a bite. Before you chew, notice how it feels on your tongue. Savour the flavour.

Paying Attention to Our Environment and Experience

Any activity can be done mindfully. You just need to slow down and pay attention. Notice how your experience is enriched and intensified when you pull your focus back to your senses and actions.

- **Mindfully garden.** Be aware of the texture of the flower petals and the scent of the soil as you water it. Focus on the droplets of water on each leaf. Feel the soil in-between your fingers and, as you breathe in and out, pay attention to the colours and textures of the petals. Keep bringing your attention back to the sights, sounds and smells as you dig, plant and water.

- **Mindfully listen to music.** Tune in to the unique sound of one instrument at a time, then move on to zone in on another. Gradually build up your awareness till you are hearing all the instruments. Keep bringing your attention back to different instruments.

- **Walk mindfully.** This is sometimes called 'meditation in motion' and involves paying attention to the process of walking. Focus first on your feet, notice how the ground feels beneath them – whether it's hard or soft – and the

touch-point at which
your foot meets the
ground. Notice the
stride and rhythm of your
walk and how your arms
fall or sway. As your mind
wanders, bring your attention back
to your walking process. Notice the
fluidity of your walk, your surroundings and how you feel.
Breathe slowly in and out. Add verbal cues, such as 'lifting'
or 'stepping', to bring your focus back to your body.

However we practise it, mindfulness is the art of creating
space between ourselves and our reactions; the art of paying
attention so we may create sufficient space in which to
think, breathe and respond. It gives us the opportunity to
observe and absorb what is happening around and within
us at any given moment, so we can regain control of our
lives and make the choices that will make us more serene.

4. Self-calm: 12 Nourishing Actions

Just as our thoughts and feelings contribute to our calmness, so, too, do our actions: what we *do* in our daily lives.

To become and 'keep calm', we can intentionally ramp up our self-care, our self-comfort and our self-control; we can create and visit environments that calm us and we can deepen our connections with nature, with others and with ourselves.

Choose nourishing actions, rather than numbing ones (such as drinking alcohol, watching TV or scrolling through social media), which interfere with the pure, peaceful feeling of real serenity. The following 12 calls to action will bring serenity your way.

'Remember...the entrance to the sanctuary is inside you.'

Rumi

1. Apply Your Calm Balm

**Which activities make you feel blissed out
and relaxed?**

It could be getting cosy on the sofa with a good book,
walking through woodlands breathing in the delightful
scent of pine trees or sitting by a lake. Perhaps it's watering
your plants? Whatever you do to quieten the noise of
external pressures and
demands, these make up
your own 'calm balm',
to be liberally applied
whenever you need it.

Make a list of your calm
balm activities, and leave
sufficient space in your
schedule to do them
as often as possible.

2. Dive into Your Blue Mind

Water calms our brains and makes us feel more connected to something bigger than ourselves. Being close to water instils a mildly meditative state, which scientists call 'blue mind'. Here are some ways to use water as a calming force:

- **Watch** the ebb and flow of ocean waves, the gentle meandering of a river or the stillness and beauty of a lake.

- **Soak** in a warm bath, feeling the sensation of water against your skin. Pour a handful of Epsom salts, a few drops of lavender oil and half a cup of baking soda into a hot bath to draw out toxins, reduce stress hormones and balance your skin's pH levels.

- **Swim** in a meditative way. Focus on your rhythmic strokes and breathing pattern as you glide through the water.

- **Drink** a glass of water slowly. The process of filling a glass and sipping it forces you to pause and calms you down – a good tactic with spirited children and feisty teenagers.

3. Bathe Yourself in Sound

The absorbing quality of music can slow our pulse and de-stress our minds.

- **Attend a sound bath** to experience deep relaxation. Immersion in the meditative waves of sound from gongs, crystal bowls and other instruments eases tension, and the enveloping quality of the sound means you're less likely to be distracted by thoughts.

- **Take part in a drumming circle.** Drumming can feel like a primeval connection to your heartbeat, while the vibrations of the drums can be hypnotic. Pay attention to the tempo, volume and rhythm of your drumming and get lost in the beat.

- **Wind down** with calming music before sleep. Listen to the Solfeggio Frequencies, which contain an ancient six-tone scale believed to have been used in sacred music, including Gregorian chants. They were thought to impart spiritual blessings, to balance energy and to keep mind, body and spirit in harmony.

4. Take Small Steps

Take tiny steps to form new habits. This can remove any resistance to starting. For example, the following small acts are enough to spark a habit change over time:

- Eat a piece of fruit in the car on the way to work or on the school run.

- Do five minutes of meditation or yoga twice a week.

- Go to bed 15 minutes earlier with a book not your phone.

- Drink a glass of water each day on waking and before each meal.

Moving forwards, no matter how slowly, is progress. If you are doing something, the process is progress enough. This calms the pressure of discipline.

5. Embrace Downtime

Where mindfulness is about letting the mind focus and tune in, downtime is about letting it wander and tune out. Downtime is also known as 'deliberate rest' or 'free-form attention'.

When our attention hovers above an activity, it creates solace and allows us to get lost in the moment, gently drifting and daydreaming.

Whether we're wired or tired, a well-rested brain is sharper and less stressed. Our brains need downtime to rest and process the cerebral congestion of information that competes for our neural connections each day.

This resting state helps us process what we've learned and experienced and enables us to come up with ideas and solutions. Without this downtime, life can feel overwhelming, as a jumble of congested thoughts, expectations and tasks battle inside our brains.

Such downtime allows deeper thought, sounder judgements and better decision-making and problem-solving.

We often see taking time off when we're busy as a bad thing, but, on the contrary, it helps us achieve more in less time; it optimizes how effective we are at work.

Here's why. Your brain doesn't switch off during free-form attention downtime – rather, it continues to process information effectively and to consolidate learning, building neural connections. Brain-mapping research has shown that multiple brain regions are still active, even during this 'deliberate rest' state.

What's more, studies have found that this free-form attention state restores and refreshes our capacity for directed attention. As a result of 'deliberate rest' via downtime and playtime, we become better at concentrating during tasks that require us to pay close, focused attention, known as 'directed attention'.

A study by Columbia University discovered that students who were given play-based downtime during their study periods concentrated better and had improved cognitive functioning, compared with those who experienced a complete day of traditional academic classes.

Our attention improves as a result of rest and play – replenishment aids productivity.

Consequently, the better we get at moving between directed attention and free-form attention, the more effective we become. Effectiveness breeds calmness rather than frustration.

Directed Attention

Gratitude, savouring and mindfulness are forms of directed attention. They help us stay present, pay attention to the moment and focus on what we're doing rather than exist on autopilot. Whenever we're laser-focused on something specific and avoiding distractions – for example, writing an email, focusing on our breath during mindfulness or performing a work task while tuning out the noise of the radio – we are using our directed attention.

Free-form Attention

Free-form attention describes our minds at rest, when they are able to wander and wonder freely even during a task – such as playtime, during which we can let our minds roam.

The best way to switch from directed attention to the restful state of free-form attention is to do something that fulfils all of the following:

- It is engaging yet relaxing.
- It doesn't involve any pressure to perform well.
- It doesn't require much concentration.
- It isn't passive or numbing.

A free-form attention activity allows your mind to wander freely while still enabling you to perform it adequately. It is something that you're sufficiently good at for it not to be challenging, but that is challenging enough not to be boring.

That middle ground is where you can find 'flow', get into the engaged zone and lose track of time in a restful state of processing. So now let's look at the sorts of things you could do to get into flow.

6. Find Your Flow

Which activities absorb you and engage you?
What leads you to lose track of time?

Engagement is one of the core pillars of wellbeing
established by experts in positive psychology. This is because,
when you participate in activities that engage you, the world
around you (including your worries and your tension) is
temporarily suspended while you enter the 'flow' zone.
Carve out time blocks to immerse yourself in engaging
activities that you can fully absorb yourself in, in order to
find that flow feeling. These might include:

- **Flower arranging.** Research by Japan's National Institute
  of Floricultural Science found that the repetitive creativity
  of flower arranging reduced stress.

- **Gardening.** The process
  of planting and watching
  something grow is satisfying
  and absorbing, and gardeners
  often report losing track of
  time in their garden patches.
  Contact with soil has also been
  proven to be soothing.

- **Cooking.** Making a recipe from scratch (one you already know well) uses free-form attention and also results in something delicious to eat.

- **Reading.** Devour a few chapters of a book along with your lunch – or, if you can carve out sufficient time in the morning, leaf through a chapter to start the day on a high.

- **Knitting.** The gentle focus and repetitive motions involved in knitting make it the perfect flow-zone activity to help you unwind. A study by Harvard University revealed that knitting lowers the heart rate and induces the same level of calm as yoga.

- **Pottery.** Sculpting with clay and throwing pots result in the same de-stressing neural impulses in our brains that we get when we squeeze putty or a stress ball.

- **Bird-watching.** A bioscience study at England's Exeter University showed a positive link between the number of birds, trees and shrubs people see and their mental health.

- **Crossword-puzzling.** Participating in an achievable puzzle can be a great way to distract your mind and make it work on something soothing.

- **Absorbing art and consuming culture.** Some doctors have begun 'social prescribing' of art-inspired, therapeutic treatments for a range of ailments after various studies have shown calming benefits from access to arts.

- **Playing.** Immersing yourself in play has been proved to boost cognitive power and problem-solving skills and enhance the ability to innovate. It's a wonderful way to stay present and reconnect with ourselves, too. Whether it's shooting hoops or jigsaw-puzzling, having fun generates energy rather than depleting it.

- **Crafting, painting or patchwork.** Making and creating are absorbing activities that make us forget our external surroundings and get into the state of flow. When you paint or craft, you give your brain something else to focus on rather than whatever is stressing you. Within a few minutes, notice how you go from uptight to unwound. Then feel a sense of accomplishment from having made something.

- **Daydreaming and visualizing.** Letting your mind wander is a way to enter this restful state. It's even better if the daydream has intention built into it, so visualizing somewhere peaceful to induce a sense of calm or visualizing your dream life to create a sense of possibility.

Schedule some quiet into your crowded day and include activities that engage you yet allow your mind to wander above them. They're as important to prioritize as the other tasks on your to-do list. Also allocate space in your day to pause, pay attention inwardly and just be.

Here are some other ways to give yourself more downtime:

- **Say no.** Perhaps you don't need to attend that party, or volunteer for the umpteenth time to help at that event, or sign up to another training session.

- **Book a solitary spa day.** This will provide an opportunity to do activities from your 'calm balm' list (see page 62).

- **Nap.** It keeps you sharp. NASA has its astronauts take a 26-minute nap each day along with regular downtime to boost working memory and cognitive function.

7. Practice Visualization

The imagination is powerful, and our mind responds to whatever we imagine, regardless of whether it's real or not. For instance, if you lie down and imagine you are on a beach listening to the waves, you'll feel relaxed. Conversely, if you imagine yourself running through a busy railway station to catch the last train, you'll feel stressed. As a result, visualization makes a great calming tool:

- **Picture your favourite place** – real or imagined. How does it feel? How does it smell? What is it like to be there? What can you hear and see?

- **Picture your ancestors** lining up behind you, keeping your back strong. Imagine every person who has ever nurtured you and supported you throughout your life, their love wrapping around you and strengthening you. See each of them in your mind's eye encircling you in love and encouragement. Breathe it in.

- **Collect visual memories** to replay in your mind during tough times. Next time you're on holiday, take mental snapshots of those idyllic moments. As you sit on the beach, feel sand gently running through your hands, and notice the azure blue waves frothing at your feet. Capture that memory – what you see, how you feel, what you hear – and take a mental snapshot to replay the next time you feel a spiral of stress rising up.

- **Visualize a chat with your older self** to gather the wisdom they might share. What do they look like? What are they wearing and where are they standing? Imagine yourself in conversation with the older, wiser you. What encouraging and reassuring words do they offer? Imagine things from a calmer, wiser, more grounded perspective.

8. Administer Self-comfort

The more in tune you are with your body, the better you become at watching out for that whirlpool of worry. Practise noticing the signs of stress – faster breathing, increased heart rate and sweaty hands. Unwind the whirlpool by slowing your breathing and doing some of the following self-comforting, de-stressing actions with your body:

Chest

- Place one hand on your belly and the other on your upper chest. This mimics how it feels to hold a child to your body.

- Give yourself a butterfly hug. Cross your arms over your chest, then lock your thumbs together and stretch your hands out to create a butterfly. Close your eyes and tap the butterfly's wings (your hands) on your chest. Breathe deeply in and out as you do so.

Hands

- Rest the fingertips and thumb of one hand gently against the thumb and fingertips of the other as you breathe deeply and slowly for a few minutes.

- Stroke the back of your hands lightly with your fingertips. This 'zone therapy' is designed to induce relaxation.

Face

- Scrunch up your face. Release. Notice the tension fade.

- Place both palms of your hands on your face and press gently, then hold a hot, damp towel to your face to release facial tension.

Eyes

- Massage your eyebrows using a circular motion.

- Focus your eyes on something in the distance, which will relax them and have a knock-on effect on the rest of your body.

Nose

- Smell essential oils. Aromatherapy has long been used to calm the mind and body because essential oils can impact parts of the brain involved with hormones and emotions, and positively affect your mood. Do consult your doctor before using essential oils for the first time, however, and don't use them when pregnant.

- Smell and savour your favourite food – fresh bread, cinnamon and peppermint in particular have been found to induce calm, happy feelings.

Mouth

- Touch your lips as you breathe in deeply. Relax your jaw as you breathe out. Touching your lips helps press pause as it activates the parasympathetic nervous system.

- Press on the roof of your mouth with your tongue to relieve tense jaw muscles.

Head

- Massage your temples with a light pressure during your out-breath and using less pressure during your in-breath. Now move your hands to massage your head as if you were washing your hair.

- Brush your hair slowly and focus on the brushing action. The repetition is hypnotic and the brush itself massages acupressure points on your scalp as your brush.

Arms

- Swing your arms up into the air like a windmill turning, slowing as they reach the top and bottom of the arc.

- Give someone a long hug. When you hug someone, the natural feel-good brain chemical oxytocin is released into your bloodstream. Hugging for 20 seconds decreases stress, boosts feelings of wellbeing and reduces blood pressure.

Feet

- Lie on your back on the floor with your legs up against a wall, at right angles to your back. Support your backside on a folded blanket to elevate the pelvis. Rest your arms on the floor, palms facing upwards. This yoga pose (known as the legs up the wall pose) refreshes energy levels, boosts upper-body circulation and counters fatigue and stress.

- Remove your shoes, find some grass and feel your body pressing down on your feet. Anchor yourself on the ground. Feel gravity pulling you down and the texture of the grass beneath you. Feel connected, rooted and grounded.

Whole Body

- Conduct a body scan meditation, sitting on a chair. Bring your attention to your body as you breathe slowly in and out. Notice your feet, how heavy they feel as they press down on the floor. Notice your legs, their weight and how the touch-points feel against the chair. Notice any tension in your back and shoulders; allow any tension in your shoulders to soften. Bring your attention to your stomach. Now notice your hands; flex your fingers and notice whether they feel tight or free. Feel the sensations in your arms, your neck and your throat. Open and close your mouth and soften your jaw and facial muscles. Be aware of your whole body and breathe in deeply.

- Practise progressive relaxation before bed. This involves squeezing and releasing each muscle group from your toes, feet, calves and knees up through your body until you reach your chest, jaw, eyes and head. Tense and clench each muscle as you breathe in and hold, then release the tension in each part of your body as you breathe out. Feel the difference between the tension and relaxation, before moving on to the next body part.

9. Control What You Can

One of the biggest enemies of calm is feeling like we don't have enough time. Making an effort to optimize our time, and to see an abundance rather than a lack of time, gives us agency over our days.

- **Plan ahead and gain control over your life.**
  The *Journal of Personality and Social Psychology* states that autonomy – defined as the feeling that the activities and habits in your life are 'self-chosen and self-endorsed' – is a prime contributor to happiness and calm.

- **Leave early.** Commit to leaving ten minutes earlier to avoid the stress of potential traffic jams or slow-moving tractors. You'll arrive on time feeling relaxed and thankful or early enough to meditate before your appointment.

- **Optimize your time.** Consider which activities could fit into the same time period. Perhaps you need to walk the dog, catch up with a friend and take some parcels to the post office – how about meeting your friend and taking the dog and parcels with you? Focus on ease, simplicity and synergy to optimize your time.

- **Establish routines and rituals.** Routine settles the nervous system. When we have certainty over what we are doing, we enter a calm state because we've automated our decisions.

- **Control external stimuli.** Our attention often gets hijacked by our devices. Turn off notifications and resolve to reply to messages during a specific time slot.

- **Ask for help.** When the day slips out of your control, regain it by asking for help. Being in control doesn't mean we have to do everything ourselves. Sometimes the best way is to invite assistance.

- **Practise patience.** Rushing never has enough time, yet patience has all the time in the world. Patience comes from knowing and accepting that not everything will go to plan and from having sufficient compassion and acceptance to go with the flow.

10. Create a Sanctuary

Our outer world affects our inner world and our environment can either invite calm or dilute it. A serene space where we can take ourselves for time out is a wonderful gift.

- **Make a corner of your home your serene sanctuary.**
  Visit it for at least half an hour per day. Keep items that make your heart sing in this corner – perhaps a photo, candle, a small vase of flowers, or a reading lamp, notebook, pen and some beloved books. Add comfort with a cushion, rug or throw. Make this serenity space a place to retreat to, where you can curl up and get calm.

- **Use a candle ritual within your serenity space to induce calm.**
  Light a candle then, through partially closed eyes, look at the flame and let it mesmerize you. As you watch the flame dance, notice the colours and movement. Is there a blue light in the centre? A golden flickering? Smoke gently rising? Return your

attention to the flame each time you feel your mind wandering. Blow the candle out and watch your worries dissipate upwards with the candle smoke. Now relight the candle, step farther away and blow it out again using a deeper breath. Repeat again, by which time your deep breaths will have calmed you further.

- **Find escape routes.** Watch out for places to retreat to. Visit them to get a dose of calm contemplation away from home. For example:

1. Head to the seaside. Waves and sea air are good for the soul – just watch and listen.

2. Take a pew. Churches are calm, cooling places. Whatever your belief system or faith, whether you believe or not, take yourself to church and sit still, soaking up that calm atmosphere.

3. Take yourself for some fish-watching therapy at a local lake, hatchery or aquarium. According to a study by England's University of Exeter, watching fish swim reduces your blood pressure and heart rate.

- **Declutter to give yourself more living (and breathing) space.** The benefits are twofold. First, clear spaces give you a clearer mind, because mess is oppressive and clutter creates stress. Second, when everything is in its proper place, it's easier to locate, which saves time looking for things and doing housework. Simplifying is cathartic and sheds the burden of too much choice.

    1. **Tackle your wardrobe.** Be ruthless. Ditch anything you haven't worn for over a year; the good clothes will come out of hiding and the unwearable things will be thrown away.

    2. **Tackle dump zones.** Go through all paperwork and clutter left on the kitchen counter, dining table, stairs and so on. Invest in a basket or 'clutter bucket' for the bottom of the stairs in which to collect random things that need to go upstairs. Schedule in a day to deal with all these dump zones.

    3. **Have a place for everything.** Give things like keys and spare batteries their own place so you don't waste time searching for them.

4. **Stay on top of clutter.** Set aside either ten minutes
   every day or half an hour each weekend to put
   everything away and file paperwork. If you devote a
   weekly 'power hour' to doing all the things you keep
   putting off, you'll gain a calm sense of achievement.

11. Write a Shopping List

Make a list of items to buy that will enhance your state of serenity. For example:

- Peppermint tea, or other herbal flavours (a calming substitute to regular tea).

- Lavender and vanilla room spray.

- Epsom salts for bathing.

- Loose-fitting white clothing made from natural fabrics.

- Comfortable shoes.

- Something violet (a colour known to enhance serenity).

- Flowers such as lavender and chamomile – their scent stimulates the production of serotonin (the relaxing feel-good brain chemical).

- Ginseng helps to relax the nervous system.

- Plants – these give us more oxygen and create a calming atmosphere.

- Vitamin A and B foods – such as raw fruit and vegetables, wholegrains, wheatgerm, beans, lentils, peas, nuts, seeds, eggs, yoghurt and milk – have calming properties.

- A talisman – an object that, each time you touch it, will pull you away from negative thoughts and make you feel comforted and calm. Use it to remind yourself of your ability to pause and respond well. Try mala beads, a smooth pebble or a stress ball. Keep it in your pocket, your bag or a drawer.

- Rose, orange blossom and lavender essential oils to drop onto pillows or add to water for an atomizer spray.

12. Connect

Connection is calming. By deepening our connections to our environment, to the people we spend time with and to ourselves, we deepen our capacity for serenity.

- **Connect with nature.** Let nature nourish you. Walk in forests, run barefoot on cold grass, lie down and look up at the clouds. Immersion in nature engages our senses, reduces stress and induces feelings of awe and calm. Woodland walks have been proved to reduce blood pressure, heart rate and production of cortisol (sometimes called the 'stress hormone') – hence the popularity of the Japanese art of forest bathing across the globe.

- **Connect with people.** Spend time with your soul sisters and brothers who make you feel seen and heard, people who help you feel like you belong and who make you feel good. The phenomenon of 'emotional contagion' means we tend to 'catch' the mood of those around us. So surround yourself with people who lift you up rather than get you down; those who offer soothing, encouraging words of comfort and the sense of reassurance that comes from feeling that 'we're in this together'.

- **Disconnect from technology.**
  Turn off the TV, the
  laptop, the phone.
  Occasionally
  disconnecting from
  screens enables us to
  connect more deeply and often
  with loved ones and with ourselves.

- **Connect with yourself.** Greater self-awareness helps life
  seem more harmonious and composed. It also helps you
  to be comfortable being yourself and being by yourself.
  Cultivate self-awareness by doing the following:

  1. **Keep a journal.** Reflect on your own patterns,
     responses and feelings and then get your thoughts out
     of your head and onto the page. This space can give
     you the opportunity to consider different perspectives
     and alternative ways of looking at situations that may
     have been causing you concern. The better you know
     and understand yourself, the better you become at
     working with, rather than against, your own nature
     and the gentler you can be with yourself.

2. **Be yourself.** There is nothing more detrimental to calm than the energy it takes to keep your true self hidden. Being yourself is a great way to cultivate calm, because you're not devoting so much energy to being someone you're not. When you own your personal space in the world, when you behave as *you*, by being yourself, you can access a higher level of peace and flow.

3. **Be *by* yourself.** Solitude is soothing, yet it is possible to strangle the peace of solitude with chitchat, music and programmes that you may not even be fully listening to. Learning to be alone will help you to cultivate your inner stillness so that you can feed your soul. Be like the axis of a revolving wheel: the spokes of the wheel are all your responsibilities, tasks and relationships, yet you can be still, serene and inwardly peaceful and attentive – centred, at the axis of that spinning wheel.

Conclusion

As we develop a more serene state of mind, we learn what to connect to and disconnect from, as our capacity for calm is directly affected by what we think, feel and do.

I hope that, in reading this book you feel more able to allow your thoughts, feelings and actions to lead you to calm and serenity.

I hope you feel more ready and able to accept and embrace the ebb and flow of joy and sorrow, of chaos and calm, as the comforting rhythms of life, so that you can live at a more peaceful tempo.

And I hope you now feel sufficiently equipped with ideas, strategies and peaceful practices to use when you need to calm down or open up.

In choosing to remain open to life itself and just to trust, you'll discover a deep sense of serene inner peace and find all of your answers within you.

Peace x

Acknowledgements

Close friends help guide us through the chaos of life towards clarity and serenity, towards safety and calm.

So thank you to my special ones – those I message when I need a calm voice of compassion; that listening ear of empathy; those encouraging words of support. Jennie, Joanna, Iva, Debra, Ann, Lisa and Peta. Thank you for being my serenity soul sisters.

Thank you to The Girlies, The Hursley Mummas and The Poppies Massive for the constant supply of support and laughter – a regular antidote to overwhelm and a warm hug for the mind. And thank you to Rebecca and Susan for the encouraging Skype chats which always make me feel good and help me navigate through whatever I need to.

Thank you Amber Reed for being my brunch buddy and Lucie Howells for de-knotting my tense shoulders at regular intervals.

Thank you Polly and Stephanie at Octopus Books for being such a pleasure to work with.

And thank you Brooke for being my reason and James for being my voice of reason.

I greatly appreciate you all.